NG WITH IT; I THINK AN ARTIST HA

S TIME. ORSON WELLES FASHION I

ROPORTIONS COCO CHANEL FASHIO

E GREATEST IS TO MAKE OURSELVE

T IS BETTER TO CREATE THAN T

LIFE JULIUS CAESAR BE DARING, B

THING THAT WILL ASSERT INTEGRIT

ON AGAINST THE PLAY-IT-SAFERS

CE, THE SLAVES OF THE ORDINARY

IMAGINE IS REAL. PABLO PICASSO

NG WITH IT; I THINK AN ARTIST HA

S TIME. ORSON WELLES FASHION I

ROPORTIONS COCO CHANEL FASHIO

E GREATEST IS TO MAKE OURSELVE

T IS BETTER TO CREATE THAN T

LIFE JULIUS CAESAR BE DARING, B

THING THAT WILL ASSERT INTEGRIT

AGAINST THE PLAY-IT-SAFERS

FAST FORWARD
FASHION

CURATED BY NATHALIE GROLIMUND

THE CURATED
COLLECTION™

PRESENTS

FAST FORWARD FASHION
FALL/WINTER 2011

4 INTRODUCTION 6 AMAYA ARZUAGA 12 ANDREA CAMMAROSANO 18 ANREALAGE 24 ARA JO 32 BODYBOUND 40 CLIVE RUNDLE 46 CRAIG LAWRENCE 52 DAMIEN FRIEDRIKSEN RAVN 60 DORA MOJZES 68 ELEANOR AMAROSO 76 FABRICAN 82 HANNE RÜTZOU 90 INBAR SPECTOR 98 IRAKLI 104 IRIS VAN HERPEN 112 IVANA PILJA 118 JESSICA HUANG 128 JUM NAKAO 134 LIE SANG BONG 142 LOST ART 148 MARIE LABARELLE 154 MARKO MITANOVSKI 160 MAISON MARTIN MARGIELA 166 PEACHOO + KREJBERG 172 PIERRE GARROUDI 178 POPPY LE BRETON 182 SHAO YEN CHEN 190 SHARON WAUCHOB 196 SHINSUKE MITSUOKA 202 SUZAAN HEYNS 208 TAMZIN LILYWHITE 214 TEX SAVERIO 220 TSOLO MUNKHUU 226 VIKTOR AND ROLF 232 VIVIENNE WESTWOOD 238 YONG KYUN SHIN 244 YULI YUFEREV 250 PHOTO CREDITS + BIOS

BELIEVE IN
YOURSELF

INTRODUCTION

"HERE FASHION FUNCTIONS PURELY AS AN ART FORM REFLECTING CHANGES IN CONTEMPORARY CULTURE"

COMPETITION WITHIN THE FASHION BUSINESS HAS ALWAYS BEEN FIERCE.

AS WE ENTER A NEW AGE, AND THE SPEED OF INFORMATION AND PRODUCTION IMPROVES, MORE BRANDS ARE VYING FOR THE SPOTLIGHT.

EXISTING CONSTRAINTS WILL LEAVE SOME IN THE DUST; COMMERCIAL PRESSURES CAN HOLD BACK ESTABLISHED DESIGNERS AND SOME HOUSES MUST LIVE UP TO CERTAIN LEGACIES, SO THERE IS OFTEN DISCONNECT BETWEEN ORIGINALITY AND MAINSTREAM FASHION. WHILE SOME DESIGNERS ARE BUSY GRASPING AT RELEVANCY, EMERGING TALENTS, FRESH OUT OF SCHOOL AND RADIATING CREATIVE ENERGY, ARE TAKING SCISSORS TO SWATHES OF FABRIC, UNLEASHING SPECTACULAR VISIONS. INHERENTLY THEY KNOW THAT WHILE TRENDS COME AND GO, INNOVATION WILL ALWAYS BE IN FASHION.

FAST FORWARD FASHION HIGHLIGHTS THE NEW CROP OF INDUSTRY VANGUARDS DEDICATED TO USING CLOTHING AS THEIR ARTISTIC MEDIUM. IN A WORLD WHERE DESIGNS CAN CIRCLE THE GLOBE WITH THE CLICK OF A MOUSE, NEW IDEAS MUST BE FAST, PLENTIFUL AND SPECTACULAR. SOME CREATIONS VERGE ON THE EXPERIMENTAL, ALL THE BETTER IN AN OPEN MARKETPLACE WHERE ONLY THE ADAPTABLE SURVIVE. THE WORLD WOULD APPEAR A STERILE, STAGNANT PLACE WITHOUT WEARABLE ART.

FAST FORWARD DESIGNERS HAVE WHAT IT TAKES TO REVIVE AND REDEFINE AN INDUSTRY. SYNTHESIZING HISTORICAL CONTEXT WITH UNIQUE VISION, THESE VIBRANT PERSONALITIES PROVE RIGHTFUL HEIRS TO THE FUTURE OF LUXURY CLOTHING. THE BOLD IMAGERY IN THE PAGES OF THIS BOOK REPRESENTS A SELECTION OF FORWARD-THINKERS WHO TAKE AESTHETIC CHANCES. THEIRS ARE THE GARMENTS THAT WILL STILL SHOCK OUR GREAT GRANDCHILDREN IN THE PERIOD PIECE MOVIES OF TOMORROW. THEIR DESIGNS ARE STITCHED-UP DISTILLATIONS OF THE FANTASIES OF A GENERATION CANTERING DOWN THE INFORMATION SUPERHIGHWAY INTO THE FUTURE.

THEIR COLLECTIONS STRIVE TO PROVOKE DIALOGUE BY CREATING MODERNIZED CHANNELS FOR SELF-EXPRESSION.

FAST FORWARD FASHION PRESENTS AN EXHILARATING SELECTION OF YOUNG DESIGNERS WHOSE WORK IS A TESTAMENT TO WHAT HAPPENS WHEN "FASHION DEFIES FUNCTION."

NICKY STRINGFELLOW

AMAYA ARZUAGA

MADRID

A FORECAST OF BLACK AND WHITE CLOUD COVERAGE

ANDREA CAMMAROSANO
TRIEST
SARTORIAL ILLUSIONS TO SURREALISM

LOOKS TELL THE TRUTH. OR TELL THE FALSE, WHICH IS EVEN BETTER

FASHION AND ART ARE TWO DIFFERENT THINGS, BUT I REFUSE TO TREAT THEM DISTINCTLY. IN MY WORK I STARTED, QUITE EARLY, TO USE SCULPTURE BECAUSE IT REPRESENTS THE TRUTH OF THE BODY IN A WAY THAT FASHION ALONE CANNOT DO. MY STRUCTURES FORCE AND REFRAME THE BODY FOR A BETTER UNDERSTANDING

SOMETIMES I FEEL A
BIT DEPRAVED. SOME
WEIRD THINGS EXCITE
ME TO THE POINT THAT
I'M AFRAID THEY COULD
TAKE THE BEST OF ME

ANREALAGE
TOKYO

REAL, UNREAL AND AGE

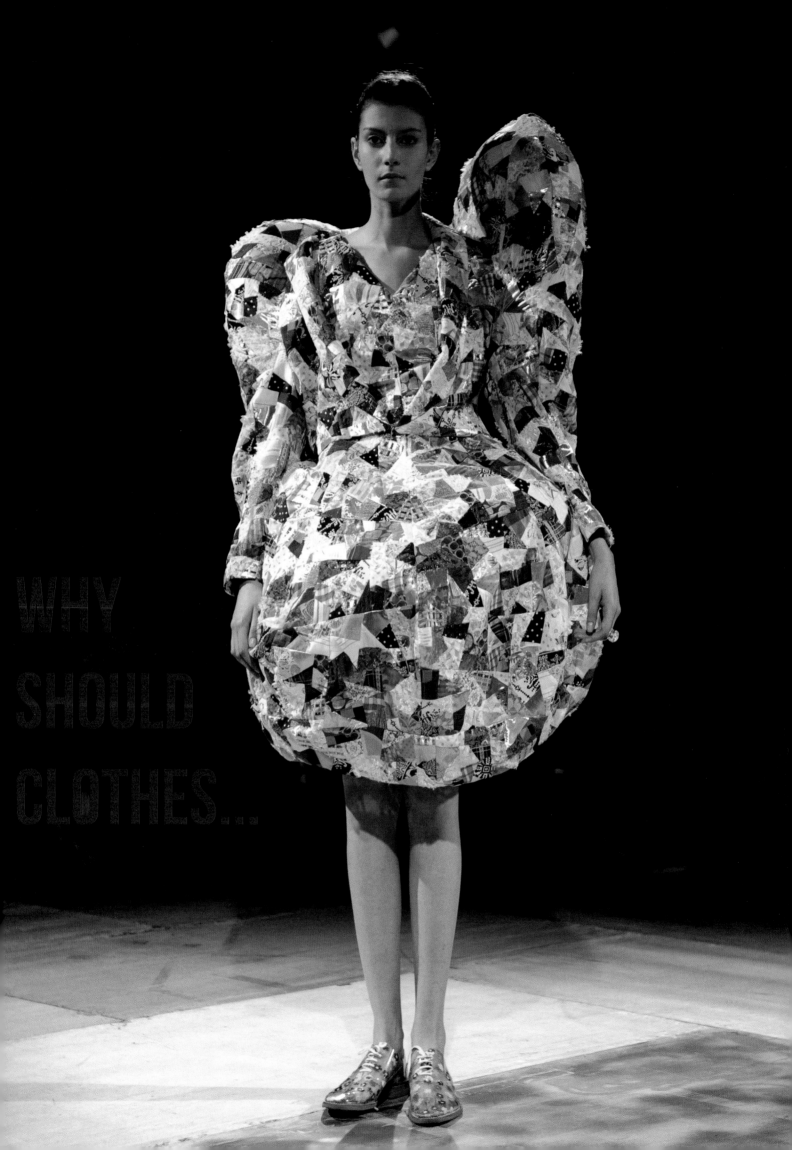

WHY

SHOULD

CLOTHES...

FIT
THE HUMAN
BODY?

WHAT YOU DRAW IN YOUR
HEAD CAN SURELY BE CREATED
IMAGINING IT IS ESSENTIAL

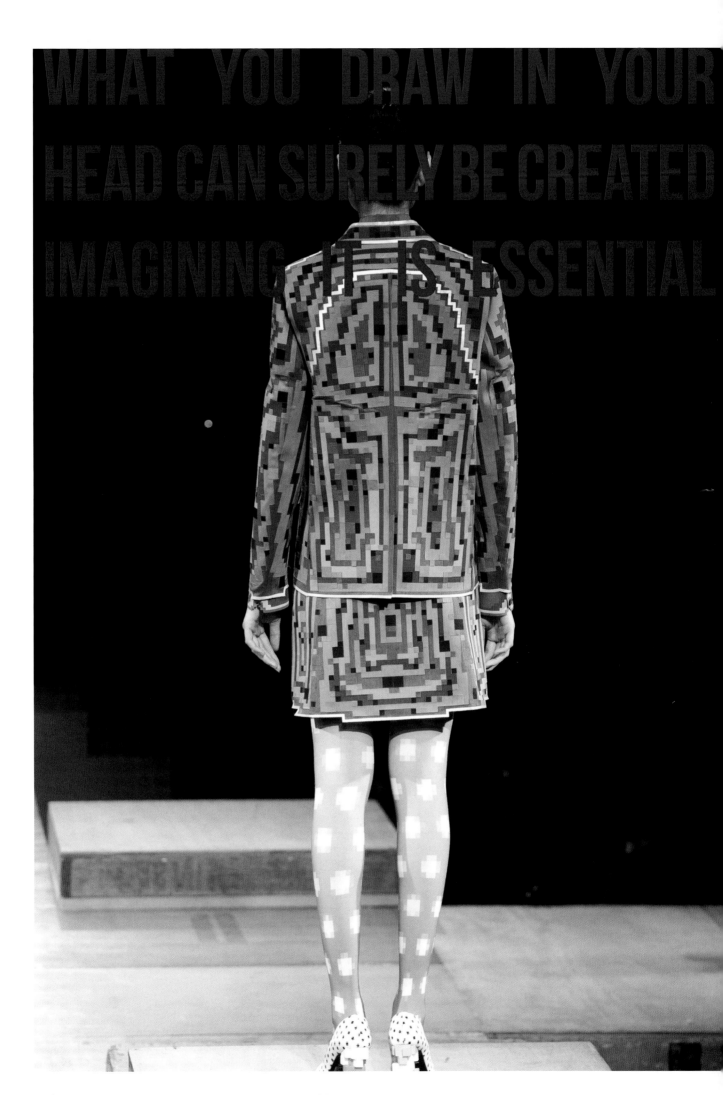

ARA JO
LONDON
WOVEN WITH MYTH AND PLAYFULNESS

THERE IS NO LIMIT TO CREATIVITY. YOU CAN IMAGINE WHATEVER YOU WANT AND THAT IS CALLED CREATIVITY. AS LONG AS PEOPLE WANT TO SEE NEW THINGS, CREATIVITY WILL ALWAYS BE WITH US

I WANT TO SEE WOMEN LOOK CONFIDENT

I AM INSPIRED BY MY OWN MUSE. I LOVE TO IMAGINE WHAT SHE WANTS TO WEAR AND ENJOY. IT IS THE MOST EXCITING MOMENT

BODYBOUND
LONDON
OBSCURE BEAUTY OF MALE COUTURE

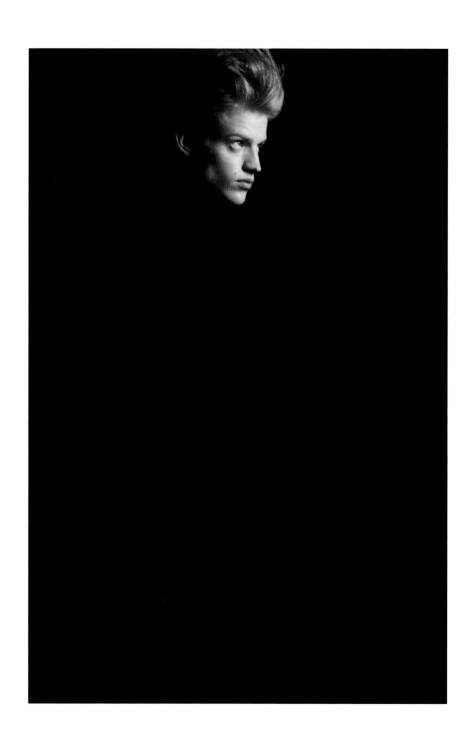

COTTON SCREAMS SEXY. IT HAS INTEGRITY

THERE IS NOTHING MASCULINE ABOUT BEING RESERVED
IF ANYTHING, IT IS THE SINGULARLY MOST EMASCULATING
THING I CAN THINK OF. MENSWEAR NEEDS TO BE DAZZLING

FASHION
IS A MEDIUM
FOR RALLYING
AGAINST
MEDIOCRITY
IN THE WORLD

THERE IS NOTHING LIKE SEEING YOUR WORK MARCH DOWN THE CATWALK AND WATCHING IT BECOME UNRECOGNIZABLE. BECAUSE ALL OF A SUDDEN IT CLAIMS A LIFE OF ITS OWN, YOU LET IT GO... AND IT WALKS WITHOUT YOU

CLIVE RUNDLE
JOHANNESBURG

MULTIDIMENSIONAL DECONSTRUCTION

MY COLLECTION IS INSPIRED BY A MYTH-LIKE STORY. FASHION IS A TOOL I USE TO MAKE MYTH COME TO LIFE

TECHNOLOGY CREATED AN ENVIRONMENT WHERE THE NEXT BIG THING COMES AND GOES BEFORE IT'S EVEN MADE

CRAIG LAWRENCE
LONDON
MANIFESTO OF A KNITWEAR MASTER

I THINK PEOPLE
ARE MORE OPEN
TO THE DIFFERENT
POSSIBILITIES OF
KNITWEAR WHICH GIVES
ME MORE DRIVE TO
PUSH THE BOUNDARIES
AND SHOW MY
OWN OPINION

DAMIEN FREDRIKSEN RAVN

ANTWERP

THE NEW POWER SUIT

I WANTED TO BRING THE TURN OF THE TURN OF THE LAST CENTURY TO THE TURN OF OUR CENTURY

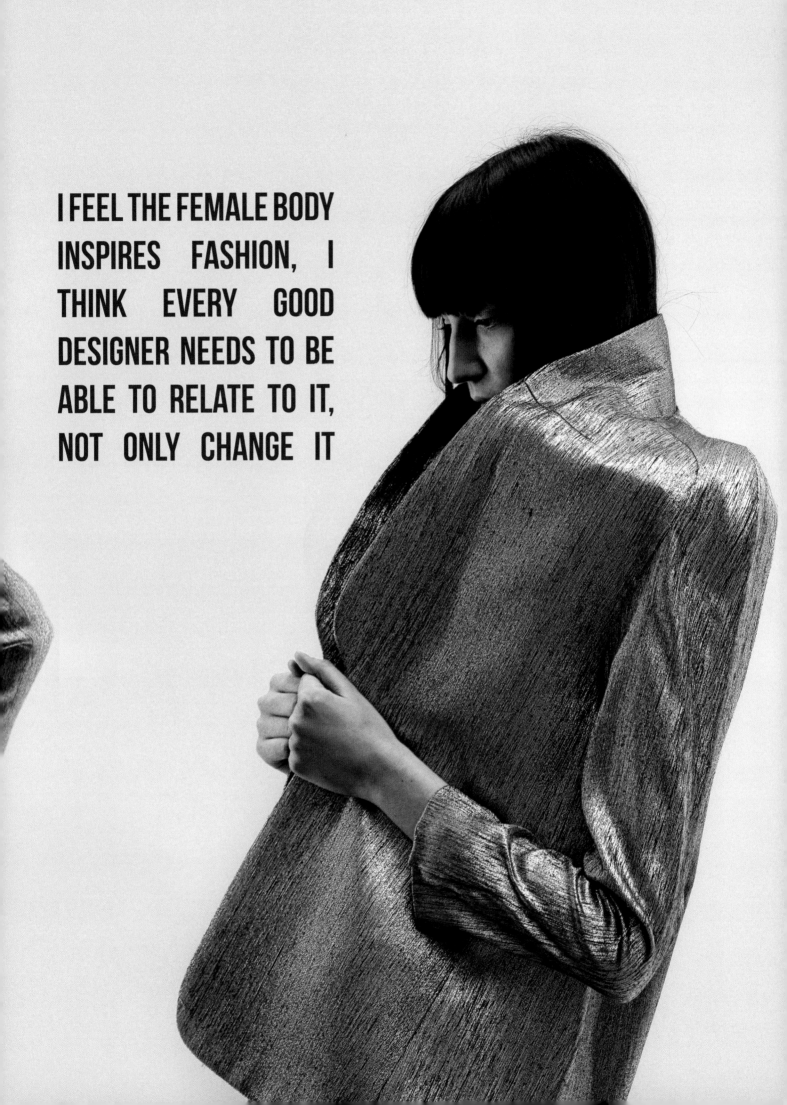

I FEEL THE FEMALE BODY INSPIRES FASHION, I THINK EVERY GOOD DESIGNER NEEDS TO BE ABLE TO RELATE TO IT, NOT ONLY CHANGE IT

I'M A MAXIMALISTIC MINIMALIST

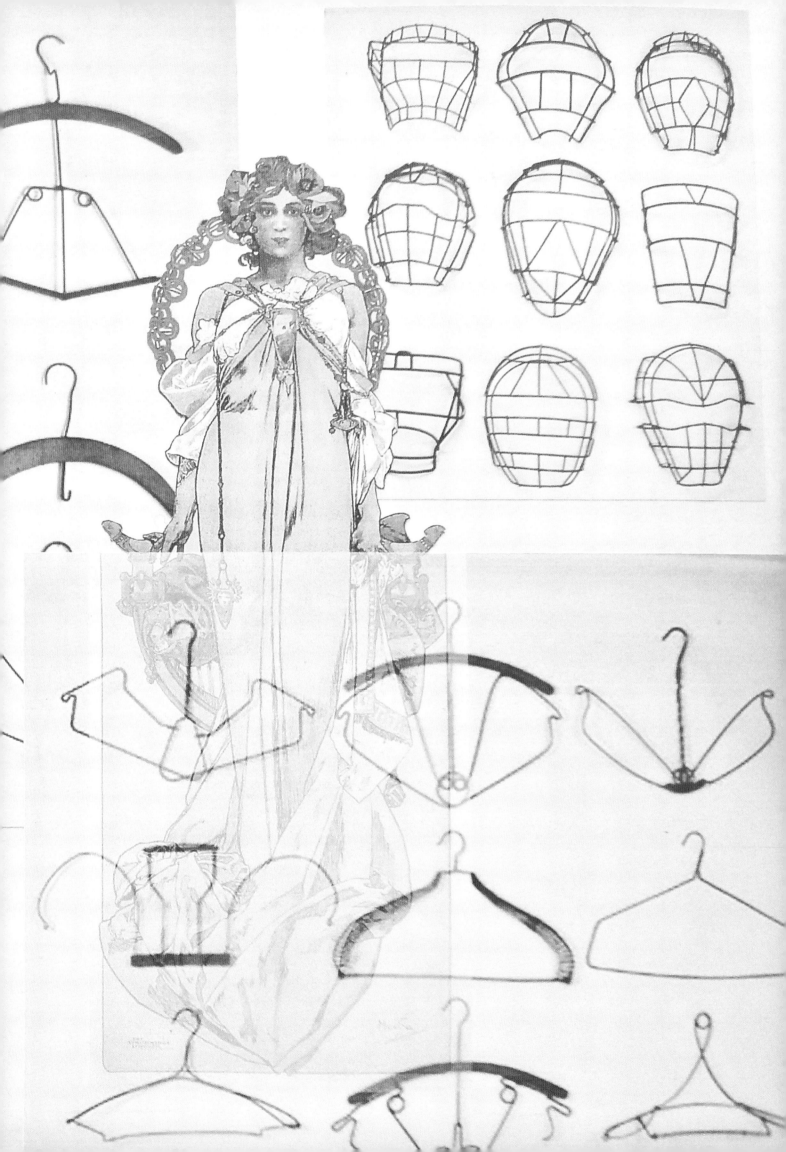

DORA MOJZES
BUDAPEST

CULTIVATING AN ERA OF HER OWN

FUTURISM IS ALL ABOUT THE EXPANSION OF CREATIVITY INTO SOMETHING UNIQUE AND UNUSUAL

I USED ORIGAMI AS ORNAMENTS WITH H.R. GIGER'S ALIEN CONCEPT. I LOVE GIGER'S WORLD AND THE DEPRESSING ATMOSPHERE THAT WORLD GIVES. FUTURISTIC AND SCIENCE-FICTION HAVE ALWAYS AFFECTED ME. THE SILHOUETTES OF MY GARMENTS ARE BROAD SHOULDERS, SLIM WAIST FEMININITY IN FOCUS

ELEANOR AMOROSO
LONDON

MOORISH ROOTS SPRING MODERN GOTH

IN FASHION THERE IS A FINE LINE
BETWEEN ART AND PRACTICALITY

PEOPLE BECOME ADDICTED TO PORTRAYING DIFFERENT IMAGES THROUGH THE DIFFERENT THINGS THEY WEAR

STICK TO YOUR INSTINCTS AND NEVER SECOND - GUESS YOURSELF

FABRICAN
LONDON
ARACHNID TECHNIQUES WEAVE WEARABLE WEBS

FASHION IS BETTER THAN ANY DRUG

MY INSPIRATION COMES FROM A FUTURISTIC VISION OF CLOTHING WHICH COMBINES MODERN TECHNOLOGY AND DRAMATIC HIGH COUTURE

HANNE RÜTZOU
COPENHAGEN

THE WILD CHILD OF AVANT-GARDE FASHION

THE FACT THAT HER CLOTHING IS NOT
FORM-FITTING SHOULD NOT MEAN
THAT A WOMAN LOSES HER FEMINITY

WE LIVE IN A MOMENT OF VISUAL OVER-INFORMATION. WHEN WE'RE LOOKING FOR ARTISTIC REFERENCES OR STYLES, WE NOW HAVE THE INFORMATION FROM ALL PAST PERIODS AND THIS ALLOWS US TO CHOOSE THE ONE WE PREFER

A WOMAN CAN PRESERVE HER SEX

APPEAL WITHOUT THE NEED OF EXPLOITING HER BODY

INBAR SPECTOR
LONDON

VICTORIAN FABLES AND GOTHIC FAIRY TALES

AS THE MILITARY SERVICE IN ISRAEL IS COMPULSORY, THE CONNECTION TO THE ARMY INFLUENCED ME

MY
FASHION
TALKS
ABOUT
FASHION

DARK FANTASY WORLD OF FAIRIES A

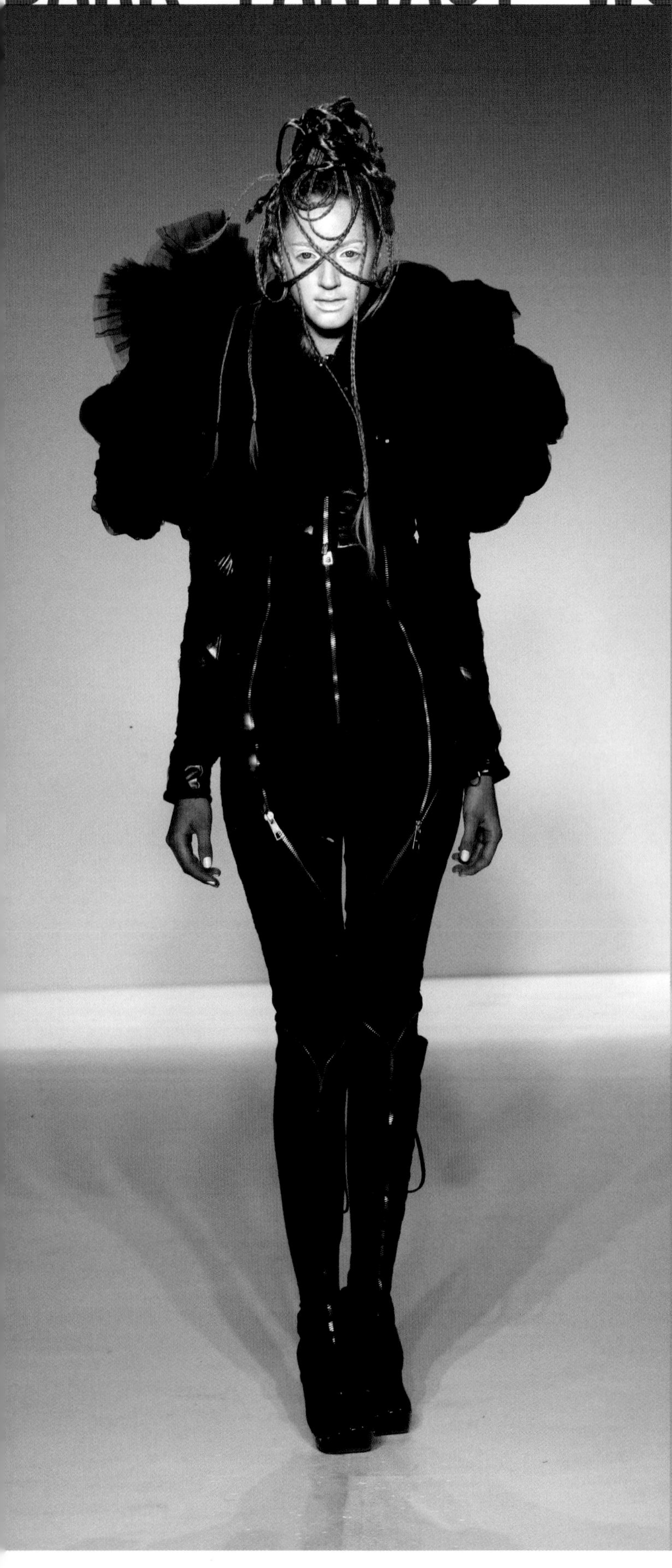

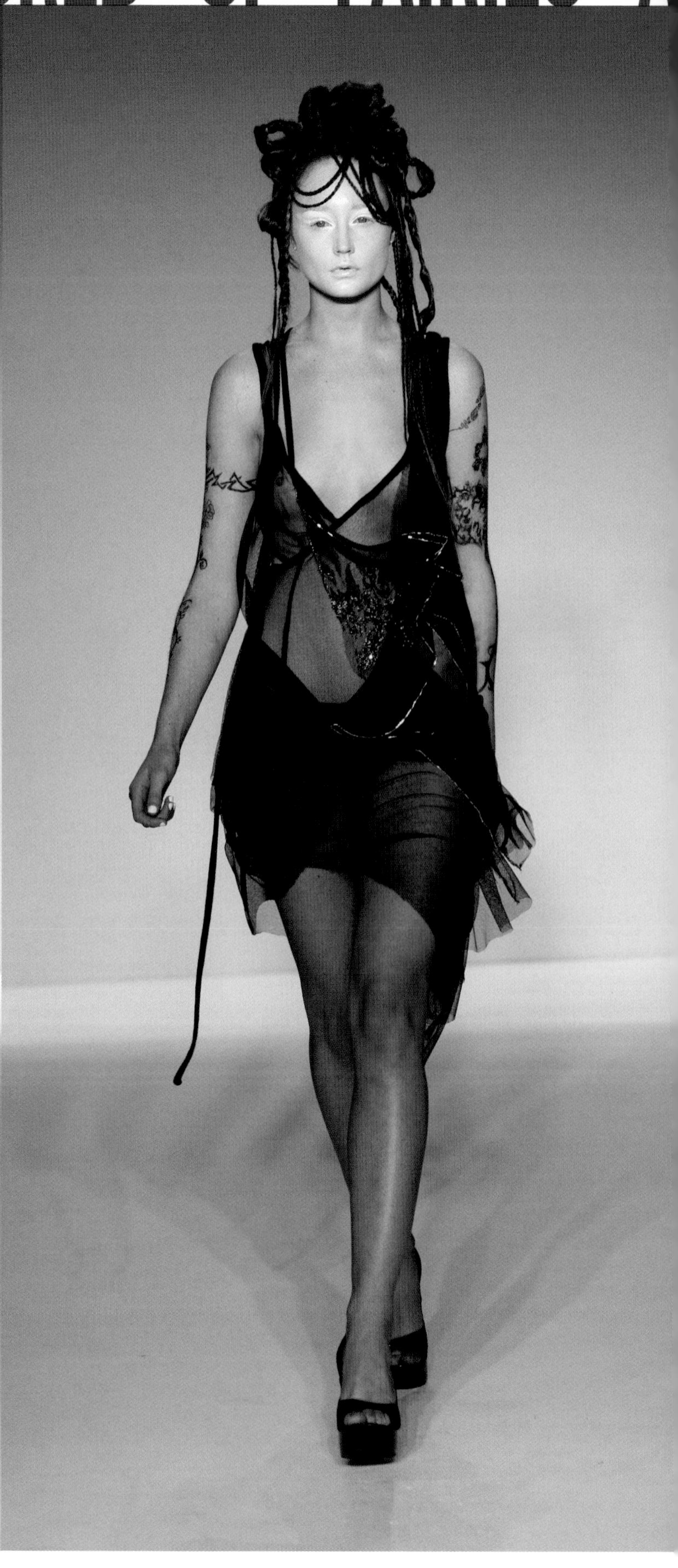

IRAKLI
PARIS
NEVER A DULL STITCH

DESIGNING WITH A DECADENT DISPLAY OF VIBRANT TONES AND TRANSFORMATIONAL MATERIALS, TO CREATE A FANTASTICAL FEMININE FORM

IRIS VAN HERPEN
WAMEL

TWISTED FABRIC VERTEBRAE MARK THE NEW DAWN OF CLOTHES

I ONLY SEE THE POWER OF SEX IF IT IS USED IN
AN INTELLIGENT AND SUBTLE WAY - SOMETHING
IMAGINARY AND SUBORDINATE TO THE PERSONALITY

EVERYONE HAS DIFFERENT LAYERS; PERSONALITY IS ABOUT CHOOSING WHAT PART YOU PRESENT

IVANA PILJA
BELGRADE

FEARLESS AVANT GARDE SHOULDERS

CINDERELLA MAKES US BELIEVE IN MIRACLES, AND WHEN I CREATE, I MAKE THOSE MIRACLES REALITY

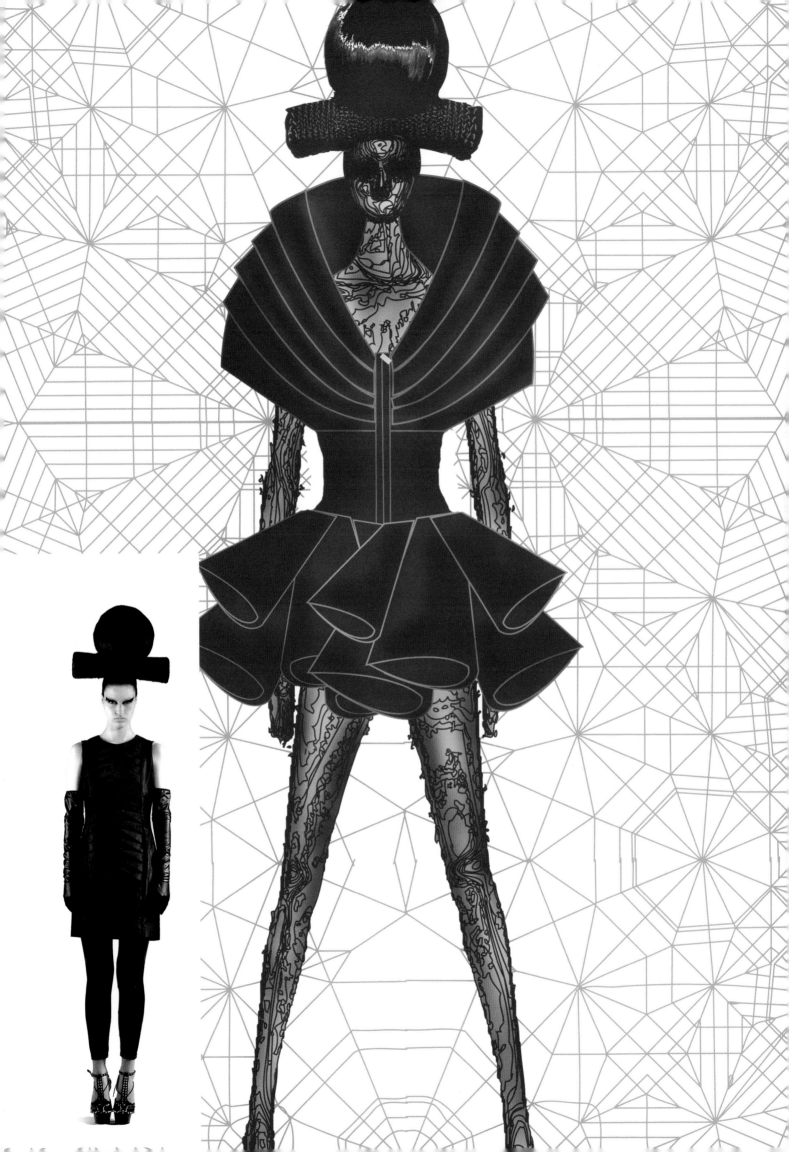

I LIKE TO APPROACH EVERYTHING I DO IN A VERY FUTURISTIC
WAY - DRAWING INSPIRATION FROM SHAPES, NATURE,
AND THE IDEA OF TRANSLATING FASHION THROUGH THESE
DIFFERENT FORMS OF BIODIVERSITY // WE MUST MAKE
OUR OWN TRENDS BY ALWAYS THINKING FORWARD AND
BEING TRUE TO OUR VISIONS AND TRUE TO OURSELVES

JESSICA HUANG

TEMPLE CITY

FIERCE FANTASIES SOFTENED WITH ROMANCE

OTHERS MAY OR MAY NOT LIKE WHAT
YOU COME UP WITH, BUT CREATIVITY
IS ALL ABOUT MOVING FORWARD WITH
YOUR IDEAS AND PUSHING BOUNDARIES

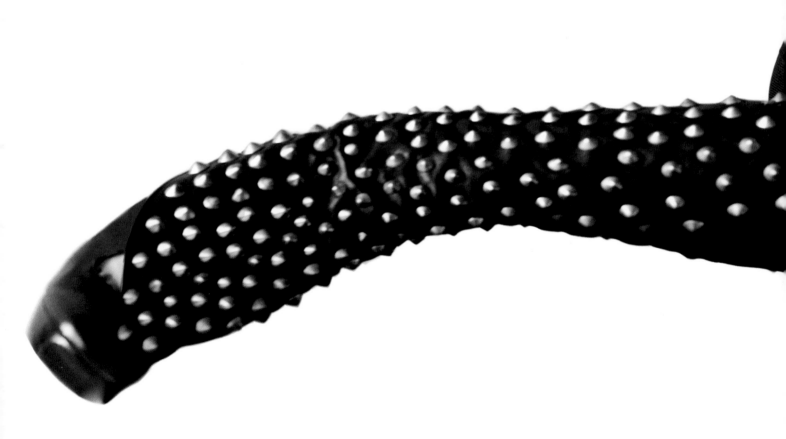

FASHION IS LIKE THE PRETTY WRAPPING PAPER THAT COVERS PORTIONS OF THE FEMALE BODY, ENHANCING THE SENSUAL CURVES OF A WOMAN AS WELL AS DECORATING IT

I WANT MY CLOTHING TO BE
POWERFULLY CREATIVE ICONIC DEPIC

REMEMBERED AS A
TION OF OUR CENTURY

JUM NAKAO
SAO PAULO
MY FAIR PAPER-LADY

TO DARE. TO INNOVATE. TO LEARN HOW TO SAIL ON AN OCEAN OF UNCERTAINTY, AROUND THE ARCHIPELAGOS OF CERTAINTY THAT SURROUND US

FASHION IS AN INTER

MEMORIES, INNER

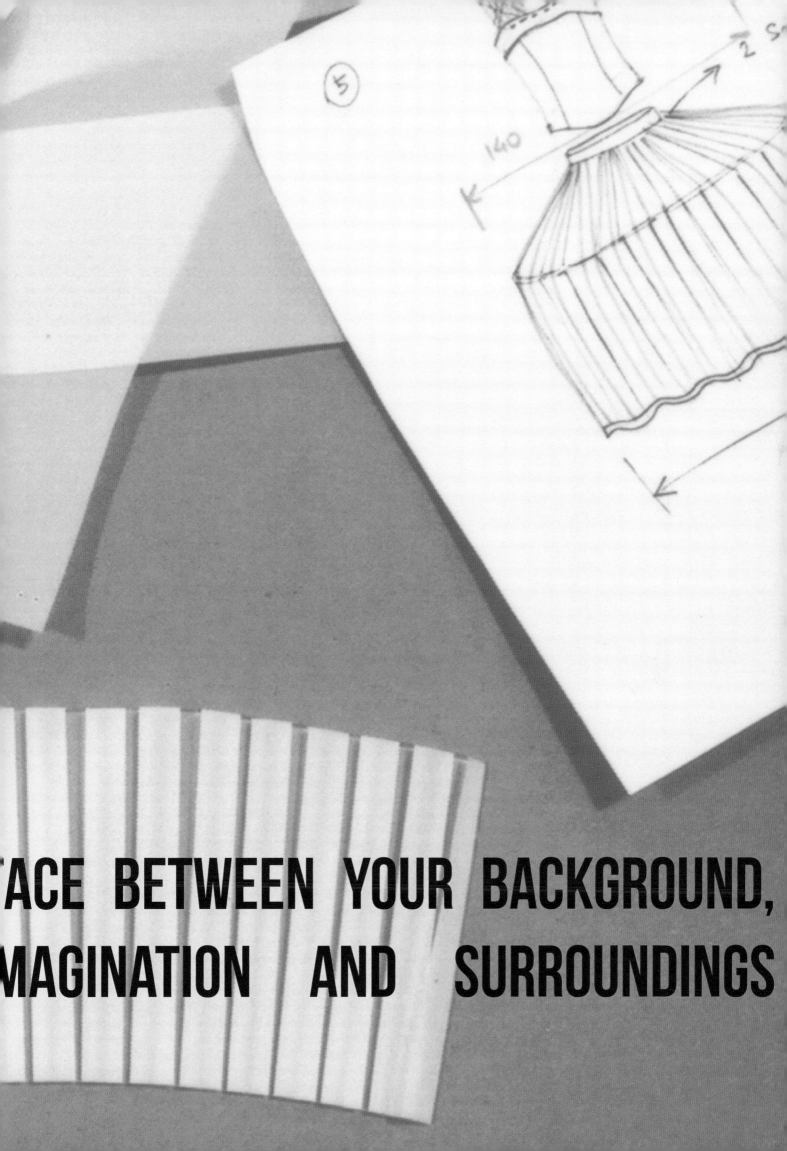

ACE BETWEEN YOUR BACKGROUND,

MAGINATION AND SURROUNDINGS

LIE SANG BONG
SEOUL
RECONSTRUCTING THE ARCHITECTURE OF FEMINITY

BEING CONFIDENT AND FEELING BEAUTIFUL IS THE MOST IMPORTANT THING. BEING YOURSELF AND BELIEVING IN WHAT YOU ARE WEARING IS FEMININITY IN FASHION

FASHION
HAS
VERY
STRONG
TIES
TO
ART
AND
CULTURE

LOST ART
NEW YORK

ROCK'N ROLL FLIRTS WITH FASHION

MY SPIRIT

CHE GUEVARA

MY MIND

PICASSO

MY PEACEFULNESS

GHANDI

MY SOUL

JIM MORRISON

MY REFLECTION

SUN BAE

MARIE LABARELLE
PARIS
ELEGANT POETIC INSPIRATIONS

THROUGH MY DESIGNS, I HAVE LEARNED TO CREATE AND
BUILD AN ECOSYSTEM THAT REFLECTS THE "ELSEWHERE" TO
WHICH I AM EMOTIONALLY ATTACHED: THE VOLCANO MERAPI
IN JAVA, A BUILDING BY OSCAR NIEMEYER, A CLEARING IN THE
FOREST OF FONTAINEBLEAU, THE WORKSHOP OF A MASTER
DYER IN KYOTO... MY IMAGINATION IS A KIND OF OLYMPUS

HER CREATIVITY STEMMING FROM
AND A LANDSCAPE NONE OT

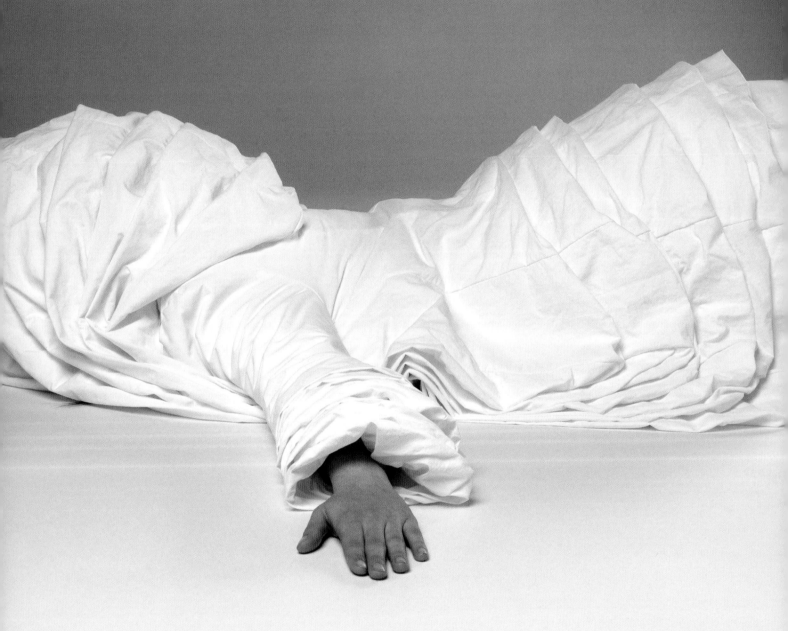

ARCHITECTURALLY SOUND // AESTHETICA

A BACKGROUND IN ARCHITECTURE
ER THAN THE FEMALE FORM

LY PLEASING // SOULFULLY REFRESHING

MARKO MITANOVSKI
BELGRADE

ROYALS AND BEASTS MINGLE IN THE HIGH COURT OF COUTURE

SCULPTURAL DESIGNS THAT AMALGA

MATE THE TUDOR AND PUNK ERA

I LIKE TO DO CONCEPTUALS. SO THE STORY THAT IS BEHIND MY COLLECTION IS VERY IMPORTANT TO ME. THE INSPIRATION FOR THIS COLLECTION WAS RENAISSANCE COSTUME AND THE CHARACTER OF LADY MACBETH FROM SHAKESPEARE'S PLAY MACBETH

MAISON MARTIN MARGIELA

ANTWERP

MASTERFUL DECONSTRUCTION

IN AN AGE OF INFORMATION, HIS MYSTERIOUSNESS
PROVOKED GREAT CURIOSITY AND A LOYAL
FOLLOWING. HIS VISION AND STRENGTH SPRUNG
FROM HIS OWN RETICENT BEING. HIS ECCENTRICITY
CREATED DEFINING MOMENTS IN FASHION HISTORY

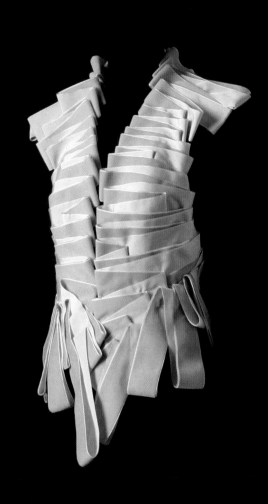

PEACHOO+KREJBERG
SILKEBORG

LAYERS OF TRADITION, TECHNOLOGY AND COUTURE

THE INTERPLAY OF SHAPE AND FABRIC, ALONG WITH TECHNOLOGY BEING COMBINED WITH ANCIENT HANDCRAFTED SKILLS REPRESENT THE INTRINSIC VALUES, COMMON TO ALL OF THEIR COLLECTIONS

PIERRE GARROUDI
TEHERAN
BOLD MONOCHROME

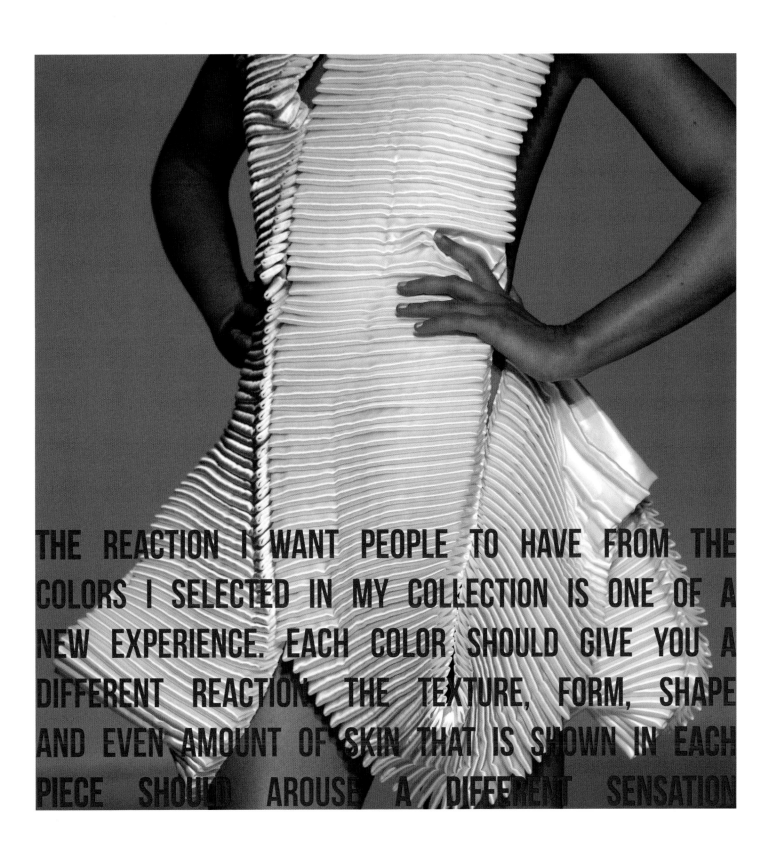

THE REACTION I WANT PEOPLE TO HAVE FROM THE COLORS I SELECTED IN MY COLLECTION IS ONE OF A NEW EXPERIENCE. EACH COLOR SHOULD GIVE YOU A DIFFERENT REACTION. THE TEXTURE, FORM, SHAPE AND EVEN AMOUNT OF SKIN THAT IS SHOWN IN EACH PIECE SHOULD AROUSE A DIFFERENT SENSATION

THE SEXIEST PART OF A FEMALE IS THE BACK OF HER NECK, AS WELL AS THE BACK ITSELF. THERE IS SOMETHING DISTINCTIVELY BEAUTIFUL ABOUT THAT CURVE // WE ARE ALL CONNECTED TO ONE ANOTHER. THE HUMAN RACE IS AMAZING IN THE SENSE THAT WE HAVE THE ABILITY TO BE MOVED OR AFFECTED BY AN IMAGE THROUGH THE EMOTIONS OF SYMPATHY AND EMPATHY

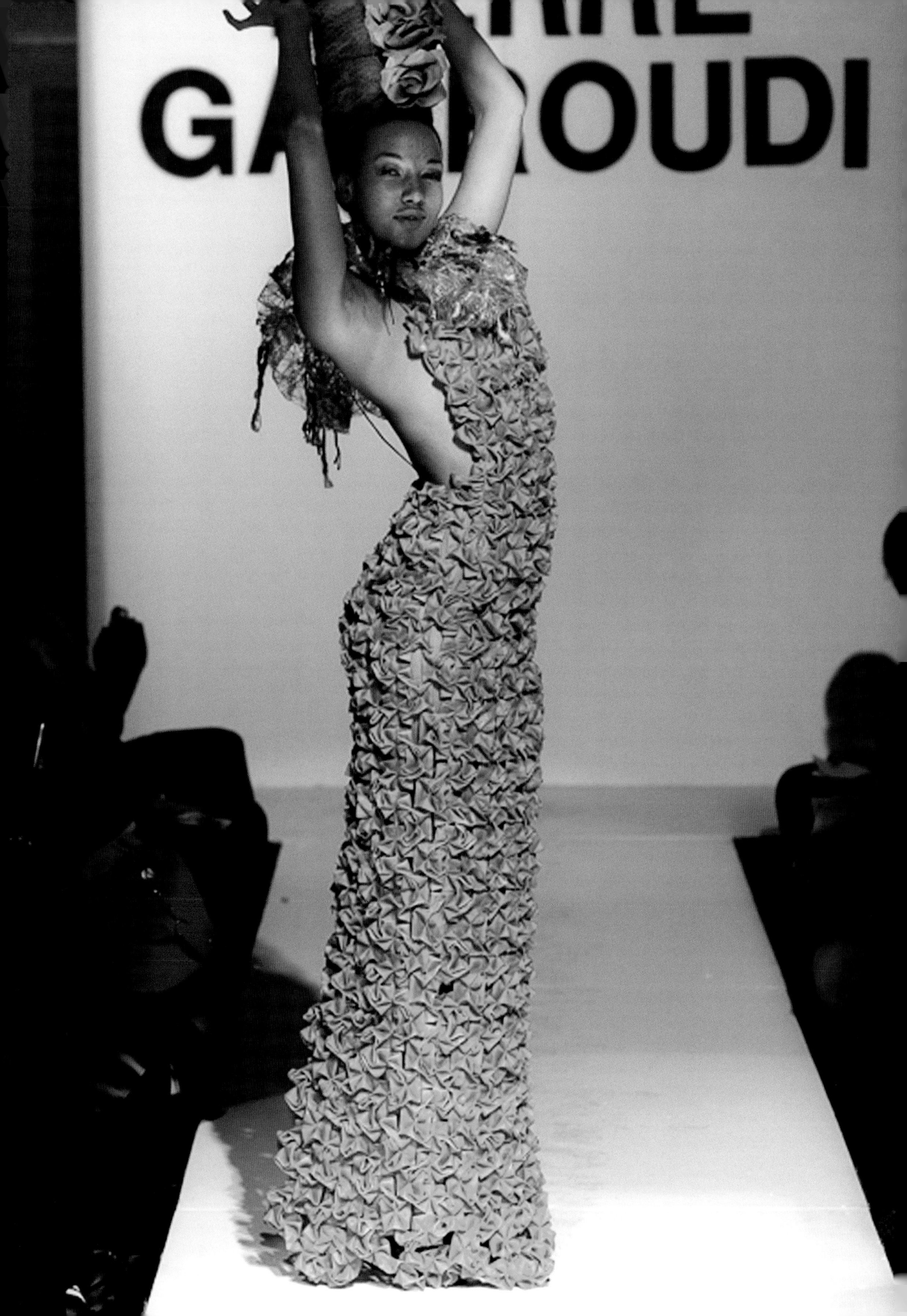

POPPY LE BRETON
MANCHESTER

MESHING EDGY GRAPHICS AND SOFT KNITWEAR

cream welsh mountain wool top

white cotton organdie

back

front

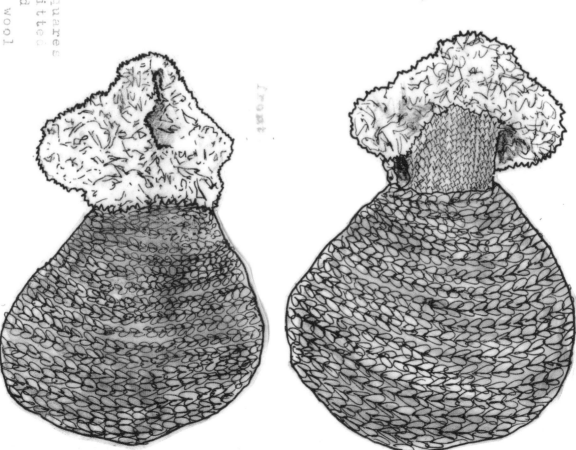

outfit 1. oversized handmade knit dress. collar. 15cmx15cmxsquares
of white cotton organdie handtacked to base. body. finger knitted
cream welsh mountain wool tops over wadding. back panel. hand
knitted stockinette stitch in cream girasol sulka 60% merino wool
90% alpaca 20% silk. inspired by a number of sources including the
urban landscape, Oskar Schlemmer's costumes for the Triadic ballet
and paintings by Henry Moore and Hans Arp.

I THINK I RELATE TO THIS ERA THE MOST. FASHION HAS ALWAYS BEEN A MIRROR, AGENT, CATALYST OF SOCIETY AND CULTURE AND TECHNOLOGY HAVE OPENED OUR POST-MODERN WORLD INTO AN ENDLESS, CHANGING SEA OF POTENTIAL AND POSSIBILITY

fmp
poetry

poppy warwicker-le breton

SHAO YEN CHEN
YILAN

NEEDLE AND THREAD IN HAND

MY INSPIRATION COMES FROM

NATURE AND THE HUMAN BODY

I PREFER WHITE OVER BLACK. IT SHOWS THE STRUCTURE OF THE DRESS MORE CLEARLY AND LOOKS MORE SCULPTURAL

AN ORGANIC EXPLOSION OF THE TRADITIONAL WITH THE UNCONVENTIONAL

SHARON WAUCHOB
PARIS

NEW FRONTIERS OF MINIMALISM

FASHION IS SCHIZOPHRENIC : IT'S ARTISTIC AND PRACTICAL AT THE SAME TIME

RAW, MINIMALIST CUTS PRONOUNCED IN THE FLOWING FABRIC OF THE GARMENTS//ASYMMETRIC, FRINGED DRESSES AND JEWEL-TONED FROCKS DISPLAY AN ARTISTIC PENCHANT FOR DRESSES DESIGNED FOR THE TRUE COSMOPOLITAN WOMAN

SHINSUKE MITSUOKA

OSAKA

POSTAPOCALYPTIC FASHION

FIND   YOUR   OWN   IDENTITY

SKELETONS ARE

PROVOCATIVE

I LIKE GOTHIC THINGS

SUZAAN HEYNS

MOONSCAPE GLAMOUR

STEELY HARD EDGED FEMININITY

TAMZIN LILLYWHITE

WESTMINSTER

HARNESSING ALLURE

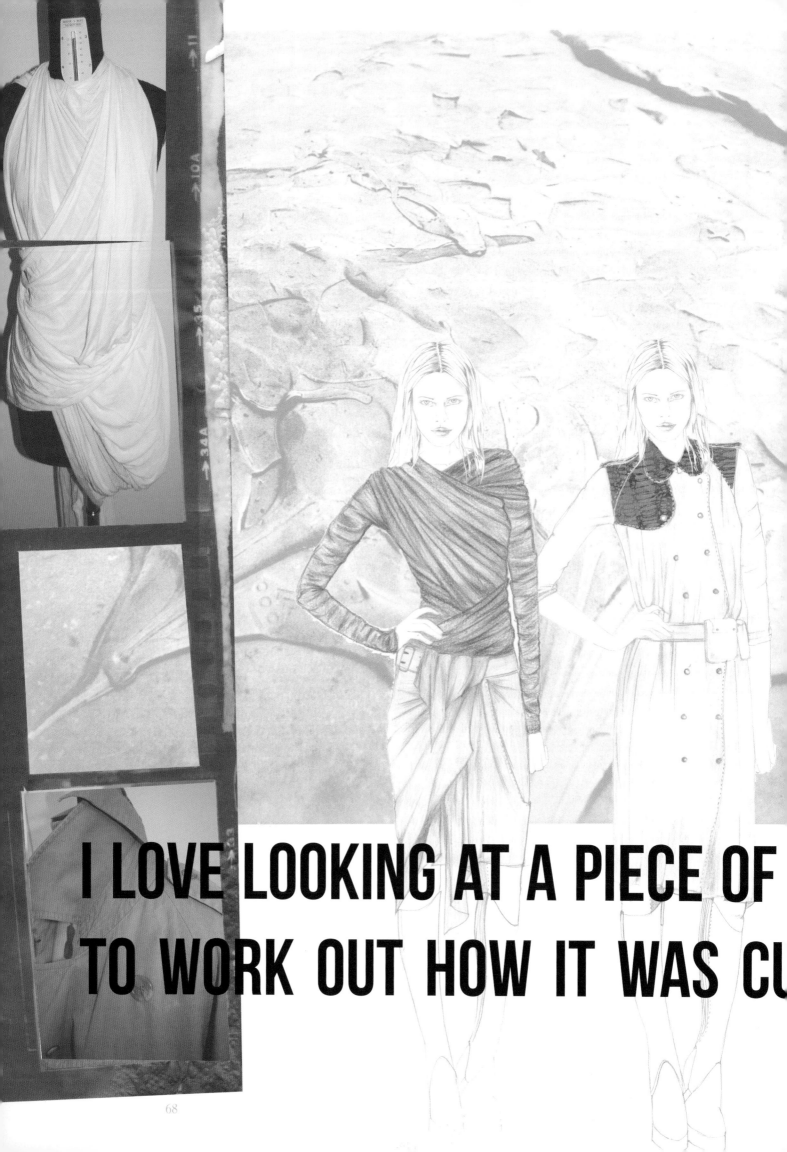

I LOVE LOOKING AT A PIECE OF
TO WORK OUT HOW IT WAS CU

LOTHING AND TRYING
AND PUT TOGETHER

WITH ANYTHING I DO, I LIKE TO LEARN NEW TECHNIQUES;
I TRY AND WORK WITH TRADITIONAL CRAFTSMEN, LIKE
SADDLERS AND METAL WORKERS, TO LEARN TRADITIONAL
TECHNIQUES AND APPLY THEM IN UNEXPECTED WAYS

TEX SAVERIO

ENCHANTING DREAM COUTURE

I AM MOSTLY IDENTIFIED WITH AN ERA WHERE WOMEN WEAR DRESSES
IN THEIR DAILY LIFE. SOMEHOW, I LOVE TO READ MARIE ANTOINETTE
STORIES. THAT INSPIRES ME A LOT. NOT ONLY ABOUT HER DRESSES, BUT
THE LIFESTYLE, THE TRADITION AND THE DECADENCE. I WANT TO DESIGN
FOR A WOMAN WITH A STRONG SENSE OF CHARACTER, ONE WHO KNOWS
WHAT SHE WANTS AND WOULD NOT BE OVERWHELMED BY THE DRESS

TSOLO MUNKHUU

MONGOLIA

JUXTAPOSING RURAL AND URBAN

I WOULD LIKE TO CREATE A NEW FASHION
IN USING MONGOLIAN DETAILS, BUT I DON'T
WANT IT TO BE TOO ORIENTAL. BLACK IS
THE BEST COLOR TO MOVE AWAY FROM THIS

CREATORS NEVER GET TIRED SINCE THE
MADNESS. THEY WANT TO INSATIABLY

ARE CAUGHT UP BY A SORT OF

CREATE IN AN ENDLESS QUEST

VIKTOR & ROLF
AMSTERDAM
LAYERS OF INNOVATION

DEMAND FOR THE NEW HAS REACHED A STAGE
WHERE IT IS DIFFICULT FOR A PIECE TO DEVELOP
INTO SOMETHING OF LASTING IMPORTANCE // OUR
CLOTHES DESIGNS ARE HARD-EDGED BUT VERY SOFT
AT THE SAME TIME. WE LIKE TO TWIST THE FAMILIAR

VIVIENNE WESTWOOD
LONDON
FASHION'S ICONOCLAST

I HAVE HAD THIS SENTENCE IN MY MIND FOR SOME TIME, "THE ART LOVER AND THE LOST GENERATIONS" ONLY THE ART LOVER STAYS IN TOUCH

VIVIENNE BELIEVES THAT FASHION IS A COMBINATION AND EXCHANGE OF IDEAS BETWEEN FRANCE AND ENGLAND: "ON THE ENGLISH SIDE WE HAVE TAILORING AND AN EASY CHARM, ON THE FRENCH SIDE THAT SOLIDITY OF DESIGN AND PROPORTION THAT COMES FROM NEVER BEING SATISFIED BECAUSE SOMETHING CAN ALWAYS BE DONE TO MAKE IT BETTER, MORE REFINED"

YONG KYUN SHIN
SEOUL
OPTICAL ILLUSIONS OF MOVEMENT

FASHION CANNOT BE SOMETHING. IT'S YO

...IT SHOWS WHO YOU ARE

IN MY COLLECTION, DIFFERENT TINY DETAILS FORM ONE BEAUTIFUL DESIGN. FOR EXAMPLE, I FOUND I COULD CREATE AMAZING EFFECTS USING THE BACK OF HAIR CLIPS AND THESE EFFECTS TURNED INTO ONE ESSENTIAL PART OF MY COLLECTION

YULI YUFEREV

LONDON

PINS DOWN UNIQUE CONCEPTS WITH CLASSIC COLORS

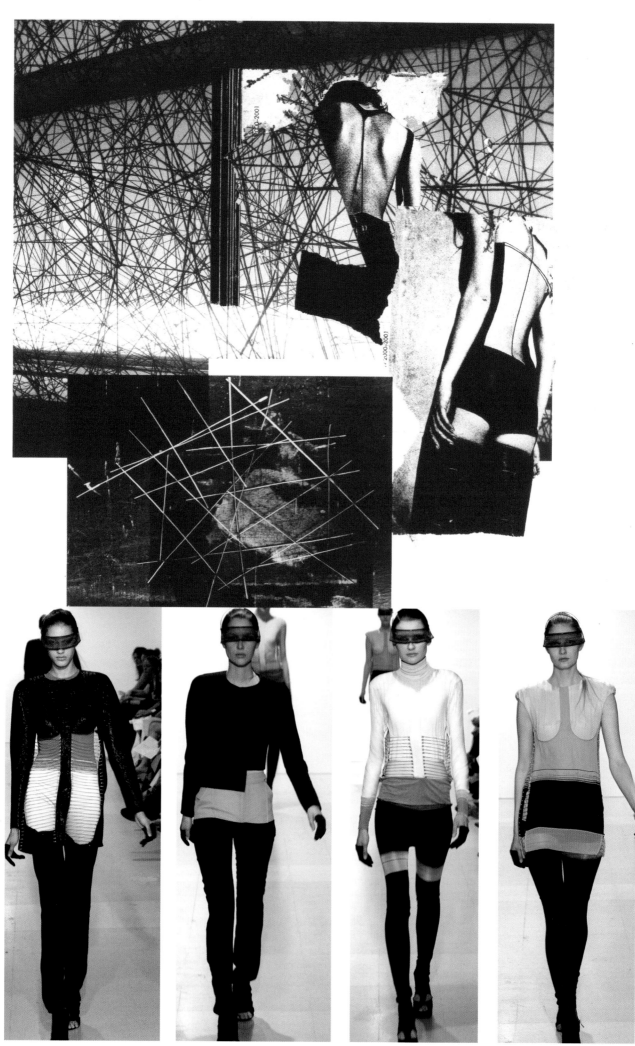

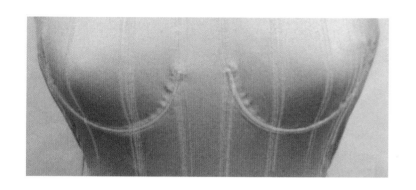

I GO DEEP INTO RESEARCH IT IS NOT ENOUGH TO SEE SOMETHING INSPIRING

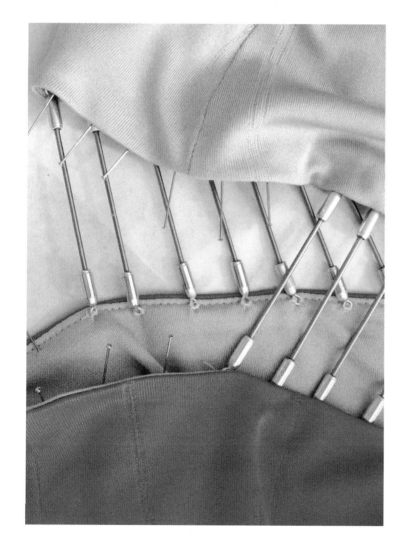

I USE SKIN TONE BECAUSE IT IS FAMILIAR TO US. IT CREATES THIS FEELING OF WARMTH AND REMINDS US OF SAFETY. I LOVE BLACK AND USE IT IN A LOT OF MY PIECES, BECAUSE IT CREATES A PROTECTIVE BARRIER AND HELPS COMMUNICATE THE CLARITY OF A DESIGN

Stemming from a family of entrepreneurs, **AMAYA ARZUAGA** jumped into her own fashion company soon after graduating from Madrid's Polytechnic University. Amaya was the first female Spanish designer to present at London Fashion Week. Her debut in London has lead to international recognition from Spain to Australia and Amaya has opened over 200 boutiques in her home country alone. Amaya is most famously known for her "wearable geometry."

www.amayaarzuaga.com

© Anne Combaz and Ugo Camera

ANDREA CAMMAROSANO is an Italian-born, Antwerp-trained, London-based menswear designer. His signature style is the use of vibrant colors and innovative techniques. Andrea's work has often been described as crossing the boundaries between art and fashion, resulting in several collaborations with visual artists as well as residencies / exhibitions in art venues such as the MOMA, NY, The MuseumsQuartier Vienna and the Boijmans Van Beuningen Museum in Rotterdam.

www.andreacammarosano.com

© Michael Smits (pp 12–13), © Ronald Stoops (pp 14–17)

Kunihiko Morinaga is the name behind the **ANREALAGE** face of the fashion industry. It was during his formative years, while studying at Waseda University in Tokyo, that Morinaga became exposed to the powerful medium of expression known as fashion. Morinaga's collections, including the latest fall/winter 2011/2012 pixel-pattered collection, have certainly allowed to him to express his ideas of unconventional clothing.

www.anrealage.com

© Anrealage

ARA JO, an avant-garde fashion designer based in London, graduated from Central St. Martin's in 2009. Barely a graduate, Ara Jo caught the attention of the iconic fashion diva Lady Gaga with her Hypnosis collection, which was featured at CSM's 2009 Graduate Press Show. Her own positive, creative muse, Ara Jo continues to dance and design pieces that express the female body.

www.notjustalabel.com/arajo

© Ara Jo (pp 24–27), © Anders Broggard, MUA Nora Nona, Hair Ryu Taro (pp 28–29), © Arron Dunworth (pp 30–31)

Kim Choong-Wilkins was born in Singapore and studied at the Royal College of Arts in London, where he launched his collection **BODYBOUND**. Illiciting sexuality in men's knitwear, this designer likes to hone in on universal truths about human nature. Kim has no reservations in making his menswear speak loudly.

www.kimchoongwilkins.wordpress.com

© Hugh O'Malley (pp 32–33), © Junichi Kikuchi (pp 34–35), © Kim Choon Wilkins (pp 36–39)

After schooling in Zimbabwe, **CLIVE RUNDLE** moved to South Africa to pursue fashion design, a profession he knew would allow him to transcend geographical borders. Clive established his own label in 1989 and has, since then, become a prolific "constructionist," his work spanning from classic to contemporary to avant-garde.

www.cliverundle.com

© Ivan Naude (pp 41-45), © Merwelene van der Merwe (p 40)

While studying at Central St. Martins in London, **CRAIG LAWRENCE** dedicated his time to creating knitwear for six Gareth Pugh collections. With plenty of experience under his belt, Craig plunged into his own label. Employing exotic materials, such as Japanese Kyototex metallic yarn, Lawrence creates voluminous and masterful knitwear. Craig's A/W 2009 collection was selected for the NEWGEN Presentation Sponsorship, and Craig is now in his fourth season in the NEWGEN arena. Most recently, Craig designed an exclusive collection for MACHINE-A, a London-based concept store.

www.craiglawrence.co.uk

© Craig Lawrence

DAMIEN FREDRIKSEN RAVN knew he wanted to be a fashion designer by the age of 10. Ravn acquired his training in fashion at the Royal Academy of Fine Arts in Antwerp. He, thereafter, joined the fashion forward label, Maison Vandenvos, first as a freelance designer and then as creative director for two years. Damien currently teaches at the Warsaw Fine Arts Academy and works part-time making handmade necklaces for Heaven.

© Zeb Daemen (p 52), © Jens Mollenvanger (p 53), © Yves De Brabander (pp 54–55, 58), © David van Oost (pp 56–57)

DORA MOJZES' collections are subtly influenced by iconic eras of human history and continually preserve the female figure. Dora's 2008 graduate collection, entitled "Organic Forms-Futuristic Expression" combines seemingly disparate themes of women's military uniforms of the 1940s, H.R. Giger's creativity reflected in the movie *Alien* and origami embellishments. Through her work, Dora continually hopes to capture the "ideal" woman-one who is confident and independent, one who is intrepid and works hard at distinguishing herself in her profession.

www.doramojzes.com

© Madame Peripetie (pp 60–61, 64–65), © Marc Vizlay (pp 62, 66), © Gábor Márton (p 63)

After presenting a successful graduate collection of innovative knitwear for the University of Westminster in 2010, **ELEANOR AMOROSO** launched her own label. This Master of Macramé embraces a dark side of design, creating pieces that combine an ancient tactile skill with modern metal touches and black tones.

www.eleanoramoroso.com

© Gabriella De Martino (pp 68–71), © Chris Moore (pp 72–75)

FABRICAN was developed by Dr. Manel Torres in an attempt to collaborate science with design. It is now a patented idea that re-conceptualizes the form behind designing fashion. Essentially, fabrican is fabric in an aerosol can. It allows one to spray non-woven fabric onto a surface, allowing the creator to sculpt clothing that fits like a second skin. Once sprayed on, the garment can be removed, washed and even re-worn. Fabrican allows for individualization of garments through personalized creations and alterations. The sprayable fabric has potential to incorporate fragrances, medically active substances and conductive materials to interface with technology. Just imagine the ground-breaking possibilities of this type of fabric.

www3.imperial.ac.uk

© Fabrican

Since childhood and by the influence of her family, **HANNE RUTZOU** has been exploring her artistic facilities. Growing up, Rutzou's aunt taught her how to sew costumes, a talent which she later showcased at the Madrid and Barcelona fashion freak parades. While a student of fashion design at Barcelona's Felicidad Duce College of Design, Hanne made several freelance costume contributions to theatre companies around the city. Hanne strives to design clothes that give a breath-taking visual impact.

© Igor Artetxe

INBAR SPECTOR was a model fashion design student before becoming a model fashion designer. She graduated in 2004 from Shenkr College in Israel with four Excellence of Achievement awards. Inbar has a way of creating voluminous collections out of the most delicate of materials. In 2009, the inventive Inbar won the Les Chiffons de Diamant Award for her Paris show, where models walked on ice.

www.inbarspector.com

© Ian Gillett

IRAKLI is a fashion designer from Georgia. For his Fall 2011 collection, Irakli has gone completely knitwear, using fine materials such as cashmere, mohair, alpaca and silk. His latest line consists of a narrow dark palette of transformational pieces.

© Jean Louis Coulombel

IRIS VAN HERPEN began experimenting with fashion at a young age, playing "dress-up" in her grandmother's loft full of old clothing and accessories. After interning with high profilers such as Alexander McQueen in London and Claudy Jongstra in Amsterdam, Iris created her own fashion label in 2007. Iris utilizes rapid prototyping as a process of designing her clothes. Her unique, futuristic pieces require an immense amount of her time, but this teeming artist certainly doesn't mind meditating, hours on end, on perfecting each piece.

www.irisvanherpen.com

© Michel Zoeter

Stemming from Belgrade, Serbia, **IVANA PILJIA** worked within a multitude of fashion houses, creating street and sportswear before taking her first steps in avant-garde design. Drawing inspiration from Japanese Origami and Fashion, Ivana's graduate collection for the College of Design in Belgrade will feature twelve signature designs consisting of dark geometric variety.

www.ivanapilja.daportfolio.com

© Pieter Stigter, © Milan Radovanovic

JESSICA HUANG graduated from FIDM in Los Angeles in 2009 and does it all: illustration, graphic design, fashion design, sewing, pattern making, silk screening, styling, photo shoots. This risk-taker is constantly exploring new mediums of artwork and fashion design, and has most recently launched her own line, the "n-frastructure" label.

www.jessicalhuang.com

© Landon Youn (pp 118–122, 124–125), © Louie Aguila (p 123), © Shawn Arrington (p 127)

JUM NAKAO earned his place in the fashion spotlight back in 1994 with his paper couture creations. Ingenious does not even begin to describe this Japanese-Brazilian designer. His 1994 "A Costura do Invisivel" paper couture collection was meant to push people to reanalyze their priorities and perceptions. To Jum, luxurious material is trumped by creativity and experimentation. To Jum, materiality is obsolete.

www.jumnakao.com.br

© Jum Nakao

LIE SANG BONG is a Korean-born designer best known for fusing eastern and western elements. Lie has been dubbed the "McQueen of Korea," and has western stars such as Lady Gaga, Lindsey Lohan and Beyonce showing off his work for him. His SS/2010 collection was inspired by the sci-fi series Dune.

www.liesangbong.com

© Olivier Claisse (pp 134–135, 139), © Hyea W.Kang (pp 136–137, 138, 140-141)

Jordan Betten does not have the common man's story. He moved to New York to pursue a career in modeling and ended up creating his first collection for Anne Sui. By 1997, Betten launched **LOST ART**, his own luxury leather couture brand. Jordon Betten has since then created couture pieces for musical icons such as Lenny Kravitz, Sheryl Crow and Steven Tyler. Jordan simultaneously runs Betten Art, where he expresses his creativity in painting, sculpture and drawing.

www.lostart.com

MARIE LABARALLE is a sought out designer from Paris. Indeed, she has tourist companies in France allotting space, on their tours, for her Parisian shop, which many see as a beacon of refined culture. In 2005, Marie launched her own fashion label. Her creativity stems from her background in architecture and her landscape is none other than the female form.

www.marie-labarelle.com

MARKO MITANOVSKI graduated from the College of Design in Belgrade, Serbia. Before studying fashion, Marko was a student of literature and his 2009 collection "Lady Macbeth," which was shown at London Fashion Week, reflects his muse and passion for Shakespeare. The collection amalgamates the Tudor with the punk era.

www.markomitanovski.com

The creations of **MAISON MARTIN MARGIELA** are highly familiar within the fashion world; however the man, himself, resonates with mystery. After graduating from the Royal Academy of Art in Antwerp, Martin Margiela worked as a freelance designer for several years, followed by a three year stint with Jean-Paul Gaultier. Martin Margiela started his own label in 1988 and in 1997 became the creative director for Hermes womenswear.

www.maisonmartinmargiela.com

This Paris-based international collaboration is comprised of Peachoo Dalwani from India and Roy Krejberg from Denmark. **PEACHOO + KREJBERG** collections consist of asymmetric layers, volume and architectural cuts. Before their collaboration, Peachoo designed interior home collections of textiles and furniture and Krejberg served as the creative director of Kenzo Homme. Together, this dynamic duo draws on architectural inspirations for their couture designs.

www.peachoo-krejberg.com

PIERRE GARROUDI was born in Tehran, Iran. After a short stint in Paris as a hairdresser, Garroudi moved to New York City and graduated from the Fashion Institute of Technology. Thereafter, he launched his own label in 1993. Pierre took his fashion to the streets with two London street-catwalks, one for "Red-Stopping" and one for his latest collection "Beauty of the Sea." His monochrome collections speak in bold colors with multilayered volume and texture.

www.pierregarroudi.com

POPPY LE BRETON is a young fashion designer based in London. In 2010, Poppy presented her graduate collection, entitled "Concrete Poetry," from Manchester Metropolitan University. The collection was inspired by life in the urban landscape. For her collection, Poppy collaborated with the art design collective, Tomato and Underworld's Rick Smith, to use the "Skyscraper" graphics as prints for her silhouettes.

www.poppywarwicker-lebreton.blogspot.com

© India Hobsen and Lee Joseph Elliott (pp 178–179), © Christopher Moore (p 181)

Born in a small town by the seaside in Taiwan, **SHAO-YEN CHEN** moved to London for the opportunity to study at Central Saint Martins. His 2010 graduate collection was inspired by the sea. Shao-Yen borrowed ideas from the seventies fashion era and African tribal clothing in order to create his silhouettes. Shao-Yen's A/W 2011 collection was displayed at Selfridges' "Bright Young Things" exhibit of up-and-coming fashion designers.

www.shao-yen.com

© Christopher Moore (pp 182–185), © Nicole Maria Winkler (pp 186–189)

SHARON WAUCHOB not only invents her own designs, but also her own materials. Lately, she has been working with factories across the globe, designing her own fabrics. Her Fall 2010 ready-to-wear collections are comprised of raw, minimalist cuts pronounced in the fabric of the garments rather than the silhouettes. Her asymmetric, fringed dresses and jewel-toned frocks show Sharon's ability to convert her artistic penchants into a collection of edgy dresses that the true cosmopolitan woman would die to wear.

www.sharonwauchob.com

© Sharon Wauchob

SHINSUKE MITSUOKA is a Japanese fashion designer who moved to London after getting a scholarship from Esmod. Shinsuke studied at Nottingham Trent University, and his graduate collection reflects futuristic, gothic elements. His original pieces have been inspired by modern architecture and animal bones.

www.liberum-arbitrium.com

© Shinsuke Mitsuoka

South African fashion designer **SUZAAN HEYNS** is breaking through barriers of avant-garde fashion. She has recently participated in Cape Town Fashion Week and Africa Fashion Week, presenting hard-edged structural pieces. Heyns' collections draw on the new roles of the modern woman, as authoritative, as the breadwinner.

www.suzaanheyns.com

© Brett Rubin

TAMZIN LILLYWHITE had a fashion debut with her Westminster graduate collection, which featured themes of English Saddlery. Her unique collection features harnesses and belts made of bridle leather. With an internship at Preen under her belt, this young designer is will surely be trotting into London's elite fashion circles.

www.tamzinlillywhite.co.uk

© Tamzin Lillywhite

TEX SAVERIO is a Jarkata-based haute couture designer for dresses. By age 21, Saverio won the Mercedes Benz Asia Fashion award. Saverio's SS/2010 collections, which were featured at the Jakarta Fashion Week, are comprised of dresses made from organza, tulle, and laser-cut leather. His first collection, "My Courtesan" consists of dark palettes and represents the femme fatale. His second collection, which was created for the Dewi Fashion Knights event, consists of a lighter palette and depicts a mysterious ice queen.

www.texsaverio.com

© koleksi Tex Saverio

TSOLO MUNKHUU is one of the first fashion designers from Mongolia to enter the elite fashion world. She graduated from Atelier Chardon Savard in Paris in 2009, won the Public Award at the Hyères Festival in 2010 and has since been creating masterful haute couture pieces. She draws inspiration from Mongolian and Buddhist traditions, often times meshing traditional icons, such as dragons, with contemporary designs.

© Tsolomandakh Munkhuu

VIKTOR AND ROLF first met at the Arnhem Academy of Art and Design in the Netherlands. Since then, this duo has been inseparable, presenting their haute couture collections with unique and awe-inspiring runway performances. Preferring to take a more objective view on the fashion industry, this duo started and continue to operate in the Netherlands.

www.viktor-rolf.com

© Viktor and Rolf

VIVIENNE WESTWOOD humbly began her quest into the fashion world selling handmade jewelry at the Portobello market while making a living as a primary school teacher in London. Vivienne then worked as a seamstress for Malcom McLaren's punk-inspired clothing store in London, creating clothing worn by the Sex Pistols. Although Vivienne began as a child of the punk fashion movement of the 1970s, over the decades she has reinvented her style, creating her own "periods" of fashion design.

www.viviennewestwood.co.uk

© Vivienne Westwood

YONG KYUN SHIN began drawing at the age of three. Although he studied fine arts, Yong's father saw his talent and pushed him towards a career in fashion design. In 2010, Yong won the Fashion Special Prize at the ITS competition. Yong developed his own brand of fashion optics with his collection, "Extreme of Optical Effect." The collection exhibits spatial illusions with detailed architectural structures. Yong hopes to eventually launch his own label one day.

www.yongkyunshin.com

© Yong Kyun Shin

YULI YUFEREV gained attention with her collection at the Royal College of Art's fashion show in 2010. Her collection displays use of bold orange and black blocks, as well as fishbone corseting. Yuli has worked with Gareth Pugh, Beyond the Valley, and Comme des Garcons, to name a few.

www.yuliyuferev.com

© Yuli Yuferev

FAST FORWARD
CREATORS

THE CURATED
COLLECTION™

FASHION ADDICT EDITOR
    NATHALIE GROLIMUND
COPYWRITER
    BIJAL PATEL
INTERVIEWS
    NATHIFA PEREZ
INTRODUCTION + COPYEDITOR
    NICKY STRINGFELLOW
PRODUCTION COORDINATION
    de.MO
BOOK CONCEPT CONCEIVED BY
    PATRICE FARAMEH

we wish to thank all of the brands that participated in and submitted images and information
for this fashionable book. any omissions for copy or credit are unintentional, and appropriate
credit will be given in future editions if such copyright holders contact the publisher.

PUBLISHED AND PRODUCED BY
    FARAMEH MEDIA LLC
    217 THOMPSON STREET / NEW YORK NY 10012 USA
    PHONE +1 646 807 1810 / FAX +1 646 417 7999
    INFO@FARAMEHMEDIA.COM / WWW.FARAMEHMEDIA.COM

DISTRIBUTED WORLDWIDE BY
    DAAB MEDIA GMBH
    SCHEIDTWEILERSTR 69 / COLOGNE 50933 GERMANY
    PHONE +49 221 690482 14 / FAX +49 221 690482 29
    MAIL@DAAB-MEDIA.COM

PRINTED IN ITALY

ISBN 978-0-9830-8314-6

PASSIONATELY HATE THE IDEA OF E
LWAYS TO BE OUT OF STEP WITH
RCHITECTURE. IT IS A MATTER OF
ONDEMNS US TO MANY FOLLIES; T
TS SLAVE. NAPOLEON BONAPARTE
EARN! CREATING IS THE ESSENCE C
IFFERENT, BE IMPRACTICAL, BE AN
F PURPOSE AND IMAGINATIVE VI
HE CREATURES OF THE COMMONPI
CECIL BEATON EVERYTHING YOU CA
ASSIONATELY HATE THE IDEA OF B
LWAYS TO BE OUT OF STEP WITH
RCHITECTURE. IT IS A MATTER OF
ONDEMNS US TO MANY FOLLIES; T
TS SLAVE. NAPOLEON BONAPARTE
EARN! CREATING IS THE ESSENCE O
IFFERENT, BE IMPRACTICAL, BE AN
F PURPOSE AND IMAGINATIVE VISI